# one pc
## wonders

Written by Tim le Grice

**imagine THAT!™**

Imagine That! is an imprint of Top That! Publishing plc,
Tide Mill Way, Woodbridge, Suffolk, IPI2 IAP, UK
www.topthatpublishing.com
Copyright © 2010 Top That! Publishing plc
Imagine That! is a trademark of Top That! Publishing plc.

# Contents

# Contents

# Introduction

There is more to one pot cooking than saving on gas, electricity or washing up. It is about communal eating, which is something that in today's hectic lifestyles we seem largely to have forgotten about.

Communal eating, whether with family, friends or as part of courtship, is without doubt one of the oldest, most enjoyable and intimate social interactions in which we indulge. What could possibly be more intimate than sitting around a table, sharing, say, a hearty stew from the same pot with a loaf of fresh crusty bread to mop up the gravy?

What's more, one pot cooking allows for social interaction between families or friends, while still fitting into our hectic schedules. A casserole or stew can be left on the go all day in a slow cooker (an easily-affordable piece of kitchen equipment these days) to be ready when everyone gets home; or a stir fry can be rustled up in a wok in a matter of minutes.

These recipes work on the principle of one pot cooking. However, some of them do need to be served with supporting dishes, such as rice or pasta, which will need to be cooked separately. Others use more than one pot in the preparation (such as some of the soups), but end up all in one pot for the serving.

In shared households it makes sense to share the costs and responsibilities of communal eating – as long as you can all agree on what to eat! And that is where this book will come in useful. With the choice of dishes in this book there's sure to be something that everyone can enjoy together.

Happy cooking!

# Kedgeree

# Kedgeree

Kedgeree has been a traditional British dish since the days of the Raj, when the cooking of India was adapted to suit the British palate. The basic ingredients are rice, fish (usually smoked), and hard-boiled eggs, but the use of curry spices is also involved.

## You will need:
- 225 g (8 oz) smoked haddock fillet
- 225 ml (8 fl.oz) milk
- 1 bay leaf
- 3 hard-boiled eggs, chopped
- 25 g (1 oz) butter
- ½ tsp ground coriander
- ½ tsp ground cumin
- ½ tsp ground turmeric
- 175 g (6 oz) long grain or basmati rice
- boiling water – roughly twice the volume of the rice
- 1 tbsp chopped parsley

## Serves 2–4

1. In a large saucepan, cook the haddock in the milk with the bay leaf for ten minutes on a medium-low heat. Remove the fish to a warm plate, strain and reserve the milk. Meanwhile, hard boil the eggs for ten minutes.

2. In the pan, melt the butter on a medium heat. Add the coriander, cumin and turmeric, stir and cook for about 30 seconds, before adding the rice. Stir to coat the rice in the butter and the spices, and cook for a minute, stirring continuously.

3. Add the reserved milk, and top up the pan with hot water from the kettle so that there is roughly twice the volume of liquid to rice. It's better to add not enough water than too much, as long as you keep an eye on it, as all the liquid has to be absorbed by the rice without it becoming overcooked and soggy. If the liquid has been absorbed before the rice is cooked, simply add a bit more water or stock.

4. Once the rice is cooked, and most of the liquid has been absorbed (but not too dry), add the cooked fish in flakes and the chopped hard-boiled egg. Serve garnished with the chopped parsley.

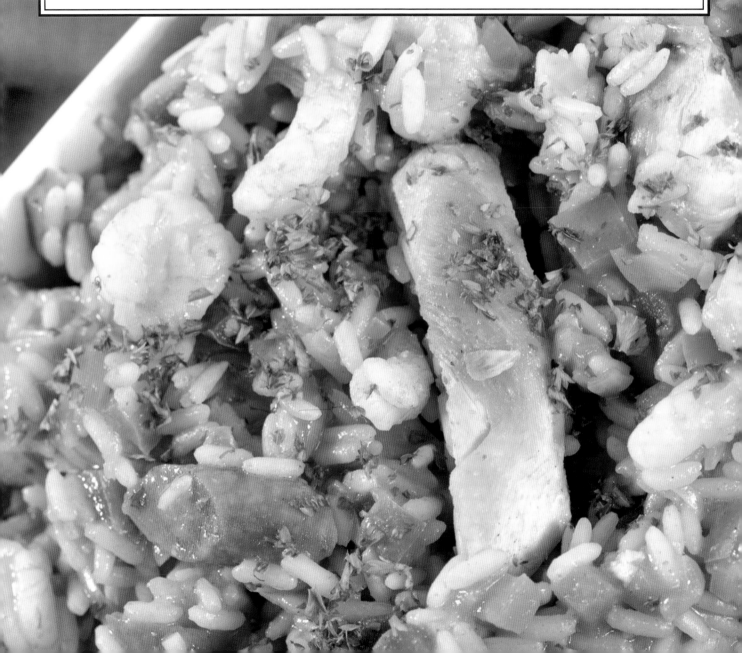

# Jambalaya

# Jambalaya

This is a rice dish from the southern states of America, and an example of how French settlers in that part of the US have influenced the national cuisine. Take care not to allow this dish to become too dry (the okra will act as a thickening agent), or it will become very glutinous.

**You will need:**
- 1 onion, finely chopped
- 4 garlic cloves, crushed
- 1 tbsp oil
- 1 tsp paprika
- 1 tsp cayenne
- ½ tsp cumin
- 175 g (6 oz) long grain rice
- 450 ml (16 fl.oz) chicken stock
- 50 g (2 oz) okra, sliced
- 1 red pepper, diced
- 1 green pepper, diced
- 175 g (6 oz) cooked chicken
- 175 g (6 oz) chorizo or spiced sausage, cooked
- 175 g (6 oz) frozen prawns, defrosted
- chopped parsley to garnish

**Serves 2–4**

1. In a large saucepan, soften the onions and the garlic in the oil over a medium heat, then add the paprika, cayenne and cumin. Fry, stirring for a few seconds until the aromas are released. Add the rice and stir well to coat all the grains. Cook for a few minutes, stirring continually.

2. Add the stock, okra and peppers, and bring to the boil. Lower the heat and simmer for 8–9 minutes.

3. Throw in the chicken and spicy sausage and heat through for five minutes or so, by which time the rice should be nearly cooked, and the liquid that's left should have been thickened by the okra.

4. If the rice is too dry, add some more liquid (water, stock, white wine etc), and add the prawns for the last couple of minutes.

5. Serve garnished with chopped parsley.

# Risotto Milanese (v)

# Risotto Milanese (v)

Risotto is an Italian rice dish using arborio rice, a round-grained rice that cooks to a creamy consistency while retaining some bite. It is usually cooked using chicken stock as the cooking liquor, but court bouillon or vegetable stock can be substituted for vegetarians.

You will need:
- 2 shallots, finely chopped
- 2 garlic cloves, crushed
- 1 tbsp olive oil
- 225 g (8 oz) arborio rice
- 150 ml (5 fl.oz) dry white wine
- 750 ml (24 fl.oz) stock
- 2 tbsp freshly grated Parmesan
- a handful of fresh parsley, chopped
- salt and plenty of freshly ground black pepper

Serves 2–4

1. In a large pan, on a medium heat, gently soften the shallots and the garlic in the olive oil. Add the rice and stir to coat all the grains with the oil. Cook for a few minutes, stirring continuously.

2. Add the white wine (dry vermouth makes an interesting alternative), and stir until it has been absorbed by the rice.

3. Add the stock, one ladle at a time, stirring until each ladleful has been absorbed. The rice may take more or less stock than stated, so you need to monitor it carefully as it cooks.

4. When the rice is cooked al dente and the starch from the rice has produced a thick creamy sauce, remove the risotto from the heat, stir in the Parmesan and parsley, season with salt and pepper and serve.

Paella

# Paella

Paella is a Spanish rice dish, related to the jambalaya of the southern states of America. Authentic paella doesn't contain chicken or peas, just prawns and shellfish, but the dish has evolved in so many countries, and there are so many different versions that you can adapt it to suit your taste. This version is a great hearty meal.

## You will need:
- 1 onion, chopped
- 4 garlic cloves, crushed
- 1 tbsp olive oil
- 4 chicken drumsticks
- 300 g (10½ oz) long grain rice
- 150 ml (6 oz) dry white wine
- 450 ml (16 fl.oz) chicken stock
- a few strands of saffron if possible, or ½ tsp of turmeric
- 175 g (6 oz) white fish, skinned and boned
- 100 g (3½ oz) frozen peas
- 100 g (3½ oz) prawns
- 1 vacuum-sealed pack of mussels
- salt and black pepper
- lots of fresh parsley

## Serves 4

1. In a large pan on a medium heat, fry the onions and garlic for a few minutes in the oil. Add the drumsticks and brown the skin. Turn down the heat and cook for 10–12 minutes so the chicken cooks all the way through.

2. Add the rice, stir well and cook for a few more minutes before adding the wine, stock and saffron. The saffron is mainly for colour, but it is quite expensive (ounce for ounce more expensive than gold). Turmeric can be used to give the dish a nice yellow colour, but go easy on it as it has quite a bitter flavour.

3. Bring the stock to a simmer, and add the fish, breaking it into flakes as you cook and stir it in. Add the peas and cook until the rice has absorbed the stock (you may need to add a bit more stock or water if the rice is not quite cooked).

4. Add the prawns and mussels, stir well, and cover the pan. Cook on a low heat for about five minutes. Discard any unopened mussels. Season to taste and stir in loads of chopped parsley.

# Seafood Pilaf

# Seafood Pilaf

Strictly speaking, pilaf is a Middle Eastern method of cooking rice as opposed to pilau (although the two are similar), which is Indian. However, the term has become something of a generic name for any rice dish cooked in stock with meat and/or vegetables.

You will need:
- 1 onion, finely chopped
- 2 garlic cloves, crushed
- 1 tbsp olive oil
- 4 green cardamoms
- ½ tsp turmeric
- 1 stick of cinnamon
- 4 or 5 cloves
- ½ tsp ground cumin
- 225 g (8 oz) long grained rice
- 450 ml (16 fl.oz) chicken or vegetable stock
- 225 g (8 oz) prawns
- 100 g (3½ oz) calamari (squid) rings
- 1 tbsp fresh coriander, chopped

Serves 3–4

1. In a large pan, fry the onion and garlic in the oil until soft and translucent. Add the cardamoms, turmeric, cinnamon, cloves and cumin, and stir-fry until the spices give off their aromas – be careful not to burn them.

2. Add the rice, and cook, stirring, for a few minutes before adding the stock. Cook until the stock has been absorbed by the rice, adding more stock if the rice is not yet cooked.

3. Add the prawns and the calamari, and stir over a low heat for a few minutes until they are cooked. Remove the cinnamon and serve garnished with the fresh coriander.

Coconut Rice with Vegetables (v)

# Coconut Rice with Vegetables (v)

This is a Thai-style dish that can be served as a complete vegetarian meal or as a side dish to a main meal.

## You will need:
- 2 shallots
- 2½ cm (1 in.) root ginger
- 1 lemongrass stalk
- 2 garlic cloves
- 2 red bird's-eye chillies
- 100 g (3½ oz) baby corn
- 1 red pepper
- 1 aubergine
- 1 tbsp oil
- 225 g (8 oz) Thai jasmine-scented rice
- 400 ml (14 fl.oz) tinned coconut milk
- 1 tbsp coriander leaves, chopped

## Serves 3–4

1. Peel and finely chop the shallots, ginger and lemongrass, and peel and crush the garlic. Finely chop the chillies. Cut the baby corn in half lengthways then again widthways. Dice the pepper and aubergine.

2. In a large pan, fry the shallots, garlic, ginger, lemongrass and chillies in the oil for a few minutes over a medium heat. Add the rice, and stir to coat all the grains.

3. Cook for a few minutes before adding the coconut milk. Bring to a simmer, add the vegetables and simmer until the rice is cooked, adding water if necessary to prevent the rice from drying out and burning.

4. When the rice is cooked al dente, chop the coriander leaves and scatter on top.

Pommes Dauphinoise (v)

# Pommes Dauphinoise (v)

Otherwise known as gratin dauphinoise (a gratin is basically any dish baked with cheese), this can be served as a side dish or as a vegetarian bake. You can make as many variations to the dish as you like. Try adding thinly sliced fennel, mushrooms, or chopped tomatoes, or, for the carnivores, some crisply-fried, smoked bacon.

**You will need:**
- 900 g (2 lb) floury potatoes
- 2 onions, chopped
- 1 garlic clove, crushed
- 450 ml (16 fl.oz) cream and milk mixed 50:50
- a pinch of grated nutmeg
- salt and freshly ground black pepper
- 225 g (8 oz) grated cheese (cheddar or gruyère etc.)

**Serves 4**

1. Peel and thinly slice the potatoes and the onions, and arrange in layers in a gratin or pie dish.

2. Whisk the garlic into the cream/milk mix and pour over the potatoes. Season well with the nutmeg, salt and pepper.

3. Sprinkle the grated cheese over the top and bake in a preheated oven at 200°C/400°F/gas mark 6 for about 45 minutes.

# Steak and Stout Casserole

# Steak and Stout Casserole

This is a soothing, comforting dish to drive out the chill of the coldest winter evening. It can be used as a pie filling with a topping of flaky pastry (bought from the supermarket if you don't want the hassle of making your own) or creamy mashed potato, or simply devoured with a crusty baguette. Avoid the cans of stout with the draughtflow widget – this gives it a creamy head that is fine for drinking, but lacks the bitter edge needed for cooking.

### You will need:
- 1 tbsp flour, seasoned with salt and black pepper
- 900 g (2 lb) braising steak, trimmed of fat and cubed
- 1 onion, sliced
- 1 tbsp sunflower oil
- 440 ml (16 fl.oz) stout
- 220 ml (8 fl.oz) water/beef stock
- 2 bay leaves
- 225 g (8 oz) mushrooms, sliced
- 1 carrot, peeled and diced

### Serves 4

1. Put the seasoned flour and the braising steak in a polythene bag and give it a good shake, coating all the pieces of meat.

2. In a large saucepan fry the onion in the oil on a medium heat, until translucent. Remove with a slotted spoon, and put to one side.

3. Brown the steak in the remaining oil. Do this in batches, rather than overcrowding the pan, or the oil will not be hot enough to brown the meat properly.

4. Transfer the steak to a plate, and deglaze the pan (see p. 43) using some of the stout, scraping up all the residue from the bottom of the pan to flavour and help thicken the casserole.

5. Return the steak, onions and any of the seasoned flour left in the bag to the pan. Cook for a few minutes before adding the rest of the stout and the water/stock. Simmer and add the bay leaves, mushrooms and carrot.

6. Reduce the heat to its lowest setting, and simmer gently for at least three hours. Alternatively transfer to a low oven (140°C/275°F/gas mark 1) for the same amount of time. The steak should fall apart and melt in the mouth.

# Cottage Pie

A true British classic, which can be tailored to suit. This recipe has added tomatoes and Worcestershire sauce, and, to enable it to be cooked in one pot, has substituted the mashed potato topping for a sliced potato gratin topping, more like a hot pot.

## You will need:
- 1 tbsp sunflower oil
- 1 onion, chopped
- 900 g (2 lb) lean minced beef
- 2 carrots, diced
- 150 ml (5 fl.oz) red wine
- 800 g (1 lb, 12 oz) tinned chopped tomatoes
- 2 tbsp tomato purée
- a couple of good splashes of Worcestershire sauce
- salt and black pepper
- 2 bay leaves
- 450 g (1 lb) floury potatoes, peeled and thinly sliced
- 100 g (3½ oz) mature cheddar, grated

## Serves 6

1. Heat the oil in a hob-proof and ovenproof casserole dish on a medium heat (use a saucepan if you don't have a hob-proof dish), and fry the onions until softened. Then add the mince, and brown well.

2. Add the carrots, wine, tomatoes, tomato purée, Worcestershire sauce, seasoning and bay leaves and bring to the boil. Reduce the heat and simmer for an hour, stirring occasionally. Add a little water if it looks too dry.

3. Arrange the potato slices in an overlapping pattern on top of the mince – transfer to an ovenproof dish first if you've been using a saucepan. Sprinkle over the cheese, and place in a preheated oven (180°C/350°F/ gas mark 4) for about 40 minutes, until the potatoes are cooked and the cheese has browned.

# Sausage Casserole

# Sausage Casserole

Sausages are one of the ultimate convenience foods, and there is an increasing range of good-quality sausages available these days. When buying meat, it is best to buy from a decent butcher. In this recipe it is important to use a floury variety of potato as opposed to a waxy variety, or the gravy in the casserole will not thicken.

**You will need:**
- 1 onion, sliced
- 1 tbsp sunflower oil
- 450 g (1 lb) sausages
- 2 carrots, diced
- 100 g (3½ oz) mushrooms, sliced
- 450 g (1 lb) floury potatoes, peeled and diced
- half a bottle of red wine
- 225 ml (8 fl.oz) brown stock (see p. 43)
- 2 bay leaves
- 1 bouquet garni
- salt and black pepper

**Serves 4**

1. In a hob-proof, ovenproof dish, fry the onions in the oil on a medium heat until translucent. Add the sausages and brown them gently to avoid bursting them.

2. Add the carrots, mushrooms and potatoes, and cook for ten minutes. Add the wine, stock, herbs and seasoning.

3. Transfer to a preheated oven (150°C/300°F/gas mark 2) for about an hour, or cook for an hour on the hob, on its lowest setting.

4. After an hour, the potatoes should be breaking up, and thickening the gravy. If not, continue to cook until the casserole has thickened.

**Variation**
Try this recipe with Lincolnshire sausages, adding sage to the casserole to complement the herbs in the sausage; or use Toulouse sausage, with added garlic.
Whatever sausage you choose, try to adapt the recipe to complement the character of the sausage.

# Coq au Vin

# Coq au Vin

This traditional French dish, translated as 'chicken in wine', was originally a simple meal eaten by French peasants. However, with the cultural revolution in Britain in the 1960s, this dish became almost compulsory on the menu of any restaurant with haute cuisine aspirations, and in some establishments, remains so to this day. It is a testament to the old adage that 'simplicity is best'.

**You will need:**
- 1 chicken
- half a bottle of red wine
- 4 garlic cloves, crushed
- 6 black peppercorns
- 2 bay leaves
- a sprig of thyme
- 1 tbsp olive oil
- 450 g (1 lb) small baby onions, peeled but left whole
- 2 carrots, diced
- 100 g (3½ oz) mushrooms, sliced
- 1 tbsp flour
- 225 ml (8 fl.oz) chicken stock
- 1 bouquet garni
- salt and freshly ground black pepper

**Serves 4–5**

1. Cut the chicken into eight pieces (you will need a good knife, or you can ask your butcher to do it for you). From the bottom of the breastbone, cut through the backbone to separate the legs from the rest of the chicken. Cut the legs into separate drumsticks and thighs. Separate the breasts by cutting down along the breastbone, then cut each breast into two. Alternatively, you can just buy ready-cut portions.

2. Place in a non-metallic bowl, and add the wine, garlic, peppercorns, bay leaves, and thyme. Marinate in the fridge overnight.

3. Heat the oil in a large saucepan, and fry the baby onions and diced carrots for five minutes. Drain and add the chicken portions (reserving the marinade), and brown well.

4. Add the mushrooms, and sprinkle in the flour. Cook, stirring continuously for five minutes. Add the marinade, stock and bouquet garni. Season to taste and simmer gently for 30–40 minutes, or until the chicken is cooked and the sauce has a nice thick consistency.

# Roasted Vegetable Medley (v)

# Roasted Vegetable Medley (v)

This dish can be either a complete vegetarian meal or a side dish to accompany meat or fish. The vegetables included are up to you, but they should include those associated with the Mediterranean region, such as peppers, olives, aubergines and courgettes.

You will need:
- 2 medium onions
- 7 or 8 garlic cloves
- 450 g (1 lb) potatoes
- 3 or 4 large carrots
- 450 g (1 lb) fresh tomatoes
- 2 bulbs of fennel
- 1 large aubergine
- 2 or 3 courgettes
- 1 red pepper
- 1 green pepper
- 2 tbsp olive oil
- 150 ml (5 fl.oz) dry white wine
- 1 large sprig of rosemary
- 1 large sprig of thyme
- 1 large sprig of oregano
- 3 or 4 bay leaves
- salt and black pepper

**Serves 4–6**

1. Peel and quarter the onions and peel the garlic cloves but leave them whole. Cut the potatoes (leave the peel on if you wish) into large cubes and cut the carrots in half, widthways. Skin (by plunging them into boiling water for ten seconds, after which the skins will come away easily) and deseed the tomatoes, and slice thickly. Slice the fennel, aubergine, courgette and deseeded peppers into large chunks.

2. Heat the oil in a roasting pan, and add the onions, garlic, potatoes, carrots and fennel. Place in a preheated oven 200°C/400°F/gas mark 6.

3. After 30 minutes, add the aubergine, courgettes and peppers, and cook for another 10 minutes.

4. Add the tomatoes, wine and herbs, turn the oven up to 220°C/425°F/gas mark 7 and return the pan to the oven for another 10–15 minutes.

5. Season with salt and pepper, and serve.

# Spaghetti Bolognese

# Spaghetti Bolognese

This perennial favourite has many variations. Bolognese means 'from Bologna' but the dish exists far further afield. Don't feel you have to stick to this recipe; adapt it to suit your own tastes.

You will need:
- 1 tbsp olive oil
- 1 large onion, finely chopped
- 4 or 5 garlic cloves, crushed
- 450 g (1 lb) lean minced beef
- 440 g (1 lb) tinned chopped tomatoes
- 1 red pepper, diced
- 1 green pepper, diced
- 3 tbsp tomato purée
- 2 or 3 bay leaves
- 1 tbsp dried basil
- 1 tbsp dried oregano
- a good pinch of grated nutmeg
- a splash of balsamic vinegar
- 150 ml (5 fl.oz) red wine
- freshly ground black pepper
- 100 g (3½ oz) dried spaghetti
- Parmesan to serve

Serves 3–4

1. Heat the oil in a large saucepan, and on a medium heat, fry the onion and garlic until soft and translucent. Add the minced beef and brown well.

2. Stir in the chopped tomatoes, diced peppers and tomato purée. Bring to a simmer, add the bay leaves, basil, oregano, nutmeg, balsamic vinegar, wine, and loads of freshly ground black pepper.

3. Simmer gently for an hour and a half, stirring now and then and adding a splash of water occasionally if it looks like drying out.

4. When the mince is well cooked and is soft with no chewy bits, cook the dried spaghetti (or the pasta of your choice) for 8–10 minutes in boiling, salted water, and serve with crusty French bread and loads of freshly grated Parmesan.

# Spaghetti Carbonara

# Spaghetti Carbonara

This is an Italian twist on our bacon and eggs, and it is easy to cook – as well as being delicious and cheap.

## You will need:
- 1 tbsp olive oil
- 100 g (3½ oz) smoked bacon, cut into small pieces
- 2 shallots, finely chopped
- 1 garlic clove, crushed
- 100 g (3½ oz) mushrooms, sliced
- 100 g (3½ oz) dried spaghetti
- 2 tbsp double cream
- 1 tbsp grated Parmesan cheese
- 2 eggs, beaten
- freshly ground black pepper

### Serves 3–4

1. Heat the oil in a large saucepan on a medium heat, and cook the bacon, shallots, garlic and mushrooms until the bacon is cooked and the mushrooms are soft. Meanwhile, cook the spaghetti for 8–10 minutes in a large pan of boiling, salted water.

2. Stir your cooked, drained spaghetti into the sauce over a low heat and stir.

3. Add the cream, Parmesan and eggs. Stir well and cook very gently for a couple of minutes until the eggs are cooked.

4. Taste and serve seasoned with black pepper. It shouldn't need any additional salt, due to the saltiness of the bacon.

# Seafood Pasta

# Seafood Pasta

Any country with a coastline the length of Italy's in comparison to its land mass is going to feature fish and seafood pretty heavily in its national diet. Seafood requires very little cooking time – 3 or 4 minutes depending on how much you have in your pot, but do take care to buy it as fresh as possible, and from a reputable source.

Live mussels can take a little preparation, but are well worth the effort. Put them in a sink full of clean, cold water. If any shells are open, tap them with a knife, and they should close up. If they don't, they are dead and may give you food poisoning, so throw those ones out. Scrub them, scraping off the barnacles with a knife if necessary. Tear out the beards – the black hairy bits poking out of the shells. Once cooked the shells should open up; the ones that don't are also dead, so throw them out too.

## You will need:
- 25 g (1 oz) unsalted butter
- 2 shallots, finely chopped
- 2 garlic cloves, chopped
- 300 ml (10½ fl.oz) dry white wine
- 450 g (1 lb) live mussels, cleaned
- 225 g (8 oz) prawns
- 100 g (3½ oz) fresh calamari (squid) rings
- 100 g (3½ oz) dried pasta
- 225 ml (8 fl.oz) single cream

Serves 3–4

1. In a large saucepan, melt the butter over a medium heat and fry the shallots and garlic until soft. Tip in the wine, bring to the boil, add the seafood and cover. Cook for 3 to 4 minutes, then check that the mussel shells have opened. Meanwhile, cook the pasta according to the instructions on the packet.

2. Strain the sauce into a bowl, and return the liquid to the pan, setting the seafood aside. Boil briskly to reduce slightly, add the cream and stir. Add the seafood again, mix well, bring back to the boil and serve immediately over your pasta.

# Roasted Pepper and Cream Pasta (v)

# Roasted Pepper and Cream Pasta (v)

In cream sauces peppers need to be roasted and skinned, as the short cooking time would not allow them to soften as they would in a tomato-based sauce, which is cooked for longer.

**You will need:**
- 4 red peppers
- 1 tbsp balsamic vinegar
- 1 garlic clove, crushed
- 1 tbsp fresh basil leaves, torn
- 100 g (3½ oz) dried pasta
- 225 ml (8 fl.oz) double cream
- freshly ground black pepper

**Serves 3–4**

1. Top and tail the peppers, then cut them vertically into quarters. Put them under a preheated grill, skin side up, until the skin is blackened and blistered.

2. Remove the peppers from the grill and seal them inside a plastic bag for about ten minutes. This will loosen the skins, and you can peel them off easily. Once skinned, marinate the peppers in the balsamic vinegar with the garlic and the basil leaves for a couple of hours.

3. Cook your chosen pasta according to the instructions on the packet. When it is almost cooked, gently heat the cream in a saucepan, drain the peppers, and add

them (discard the balsamic vinegar). Stir for a minute, until the peppers are warmed through and the cream has thickened slightly. Add fresh black pepper and stir in the pasta of your choice. Serve with a green salad.

# Smoked Haddock with Tagliatelle

# Smoked Haddock with Tagliatelle

The firm, flaky texture of smoked haddock lends itself perfectly to this type of cooking, as it will break up nicely into the sauce, but not disintegrate completely. When buying smoked haddock, try to buy undyed fish. The luminous yellow dye that some smoke houses use is totally unnecessary.

You will need:
- 25 g (1 oz) unsalted butter
- 2 shallots, finely chopped
- 1 tbsp flour
- 450 ml (16 fl.oz) milk
- 450 g (1 lb) undyed smoked haddock fillets, skinned and cut into chunks
- 100 g (3½ oz) dried tagliatelle
- freshly ground black pepper
- a handful of freshly chopped parsley

Serves 3–4

1. Over a medium heat, melt the butter in a large saucepan and fry the shallots until softened. Add the flour, and cook gently for a few minutes, stirring constantly.

2. Carefully add the milk, a little at a time, stirring all the time. The sauce will thicken as the milk warms up – this is a basic béchamel sauce.

3. Add the smoked haddock and simmer gently for about ten minutes, until the fish is cooked and beginning to fall apart slightly. Meanwhile, cook the tagliatelle in boiling, salted water.

4. Taste the sauce and season with the black pepper, stir in the chopped parsley and serve over your freshly cooked tagliatelle.

# Spicy Tuna with Penne

# Spicy Tuna with Penne

Tinned tuna is perfectly acceptable for this sauce, though of course you could use fresh tuna if you're feeling extravagant. However, take care not to overcook fresh tuna as it becomes very dry, even in a sauce.

**You will need:**
- 100 g (3½ oz) dried penne pasta quills
- 2 shallots, finely chopped
- 2 garlic cloves, crushed
- 1 tbsp olive oil
- 100 g (3½ oz) mushrooms, sliced
- 1 red pepper, diced
- 230 g (8 oz) tinned chopped tomatoes
- 200 g (7 oz) tinned tuna
- 2 generous shakes of chilli sauce
- loads of freshly ground black pepper

Serves 3–4

1. Cook the penne according to the instructions on the packet, but turn off the heat two minutes before the pasta is cooked. Drain the pasta and set aside.

2. In a large pan, fry the shallots and garlic in the oil over a medium heat until softened. Add the mushrooms and chopped pepper and stir-fry for about five minutes.

3. Add the tomatoes, and bring up to a gentle simmer, and cook until the sauce has thickened.

4. Add the tuna, chilli sauce and black pepper, and stir in. Cook for a couple of minutes.

5. Meanwhile, rinse your cooked pasta with boiling water. Add to the pan, stir, heat through, and serve.

# Stocks

# Chicken Stock

Chicken stock is an excellent base for sauces and soups. It is also good for flavouring dishes such as risotto.

**You will need:**
- 450 g (1 lb) chicken bones
- 1 large onion, quartered with the skin left on
- 2 carrots, roughly chopped
- 1 celery stick, chopped
- 5 or 6 black peppercorns
- 5 cloves
- 4 bay leaves

1. Place all the ingredients in the largest saucepan or stockpot you have, cover with cold water and bring to the boil.

2. Lower the heat, skim any scum from the surface with a slotted spoon and simmer until the water has reduced by half. Top up with water again and reduce by half once more.

3. Strain the stock. Once cooled, store in the fridge until needed, or freeze in a suitable container.

# Brown Stock

Brown stock can be made from beef, chicken or lamb bones that have first been roasted to give the stock its colour and intense flavour. It can be used for all manner of soups and sauces and is well worth the effort. When having beef for a Sunday roast, buy rib of beef on the bone. The bone can be used to make the stock for a soup, or as a base for the gravy for next week's roast. Likewise with lamb and chicken. Never throw those bones out. There is so much you can do with the stock you make from them.

## You will need:
- 450 g (1 lb) bones, as meaty as possible
- 150 ml (5 fl.oz) red wine
- 1 large onion, skin left on and quartered
- 1 carrot, chopped
- 1 celery stick, chopped
- 5 or 6 black peppercorns
- 5 cloves
- 4 bay leaves

1. Preheat the oven to 180°C/ 350°F/gas mark 4 and, in a roasting pan, roast the bones for about 20 minutes, or until nicely browned.

2. Remove the bones, and deglaze the pan (see opposite) with the wine. Put these juices, with the bones and the rest of the ingredients in the largest stockpot you have.

3. Cover with cold water, bring to the boil, skim, and proceed as for chicken stock (p. 42), reducing and topping up with more water. The more times you can repeat this reducing and topping up procedure, the more flavoursome the stock will be. When made properly, it should set to a jelly when refrigerated.

## Deglazing the pan:

This is an excellent way of using the rich flavour of cooking meats in your sauces and stocks. It is usually done with alcohol, as this will pick up the juices more effectively than just using water. Pour the liquid into the pan and, over a low heat, stir up all the gunky bits in the bottom of the pan to form a nice rich liquor that can then be added to your dish.

# Fish Stock

Use fresh, raw fish bones for fish stock, and be particularly careful not to boil the stock too vigorously or for too long as it will become cloudy and bitter. If you have a local fishmonger or fish stall on a local market, buy prawns in their shells as these make fantastic stock. Fish heads can be used too, but make sure you rinse them to remove any blood and remove the inside of the gills, as this will also make the stock bitter. The best way to get fish bones is to buy whole fish and fillet them yourself, or ask the fishmonger to fillet them for you, but tell him you want to keep the bones.

The method for making fish stock is the same as for chicken stock (p. 42). Combine the fish bones, onions, vegetables, herbs, spices and water, but don't roast the bones or top up with water to repeat the reduction process. One reduction is enough.

# Vegetable Stock (v)

This vegetable stock is used for poaching fish and preparing vegetarian soups and sauces.

Again, the basic principles of stock-making apply. Simmer any vegetables of your choice (onions, carrots, celery, broccoli stalks etc) with herbs and spices (bay leaves, peppercorns, cloves etc) to make a flavoured liquor. A glass or two of white wine can be added as well to add a bit more interest. As with meat stocks, reducing the concoction down and topping up the liquid will intensify the flavour.

# Cream of Chicken and Mushroom Soup

# Cream of Chicken and Mushroom Soup

This is a perfect supper for a Monday evening if you've had roast chicken for Sunday lunch and you've got some meat left on the bones. You don't need any stock in reserve as you're going to make it there and then. Of course the recipe will work with pre-prepared stock too.

**You will need:**

- 1 chicken carcass, as meaty as possible
- 1 onion, quartered
- 1 carrot, chopped
- 1 celery stick, chopped
- 5 or 6 black peppercorns
- 4 cloves
- 3 or 4 bay leaves
- 100 g (3½ oz) mushrooms
- 25 g (1 oz) butter
- 25 g (1 oz) flour
- 225 ml (8 fl.oz) double cream
- salt and black pepper
- fresh parsley (optional)

**Serves 4**

1. Make a quick stock by putting the chicken, onion, carrot, celery, peppercorns, cloves and bay leaves in a large saucepan. Cover with about a litre (1¾ pt) cold water and bring to the boil. Simmer gently for about twenty minutes.

2. Strain the stock and remove the bones. Pick the meat off the bones and put this to one side. Return all the stock ingredients to the pan and continue to simmer for half an hour or so until the liquid has reduced by half.

3. Meanwhile, slice and gently fry the mushrooms in the butter in a large pan. You can keep the mushrooms on a low heat for up to twenty minutes, during which time their flavour will develop. Add the flour, stir well and cook for a few minutes to make a 'roux' (a butter-flour mix).

4. Strain the stock once more and add it slowly to the pan containing the mushrooms and roux, stirring constantly.

5. Add the reserved chicken meat and cook gently for about ten minutes. Add the cream and stir it in. Season to taste with salt and pepper and serve garnished with the fresh parsley if desired.

# Cock-a-Leekie Soup

# Cock-a-Leekie Soup

This soup is a traditional Welsh dish, using their national symbol, the leek. It is a thick soup, using potatoes as the thickening agent, and is a meal in itself when served with a hunk of crusty bread.

## You will need:
- 1 litre (1¾ pt) chicken stock (see p. 42)
- 2 large potatoes, peeled and diced
- 2 carrots, finely diced
- 1 large leek, cleaned and shredded
- 50 g (2 oz) butter
- 2 chicken breast fillets, or 450 g (16 oz) sliced, cooked chicken
- salt and lots of freshly ground black pepper

## Serves 4–6

1. Put the stock and the potatoes in a saucepan and bring to the boil. Simmer until the potatoes are cooked, and then blend until smooth in a food processor.

2. In your soup pan, fry the carrots and the leek in the butter for about ten minutes over a medium-low heat. Add the chicken and fry for a few minutes more until browned.

3. Add the stock and potato mix, stir and bring back to a gentle simmer. Cook for a further 12–15 minutes or until the chicken is cooked or heated through and the vegetables are tender.

4. Season with salt and pepper, and serve.

# Fish Chowder

# Fish Chowder

Chowder is an American term for a soup, normally based on fish or shellfish and usually, but not always, containing milk. Any white fish can be used, but smoked haddock works particularly well. You could also try throwing in a few mussels, clams or prawns if you like.

**You will need:**
- I large potato
- 50 g (2 oz) butter
- I onion, finely chopped
- 2 garlic cloves, crushed
- 400 g (14 oz) tinned tomatoes
- 450 ml (16 fl.oz) fish stock
- 2 bay leaves
- 225 ml (8 fl.oz) milk
- 450 g (1 lb) white fish, filleted, boned and cut into bite-size chunks
- a pinch cayenne
- salt and black pepper
- fresh parsley to garnish (optional)

**Serves 4**

1. Cut the potato into large cubes. In a soup pan, melt the butter over a low heat and gently fry the onions, garlic and diced potato until the potato is tender (you want the potato to break up and thicken the soup).

2. Add the tomatoes, stock and bay leaves and simmer for about ten minutes or until the soup starts to thicken. Add the milk and return to a simmer.

3. Add the fish. Gently simmer for about ten minutes, add the cayenne, salt and pepper to taste and serve garnished with fresh parsley if desired.

# Thai Soup with Pork and Noodles

# Thai Soup with Pork and Noodles

Thai people are very fond of soups, which are normally thin, highly spiced and served with noodles. Thai dishes tend to combine contrasting tastes, so this soup contains the sweetness of coconut milk and cane sugar, the fiery heat of chillies, the sour bite of limes and the freshness of lemongrass, ginger and coriander leaves.

**You will need:**
- 2 shallots
- 4 or 5 red bird's-eye chillies
- a thumb-sized piece of ginger
- 4 garlic cloves
- 1 lemongrass stalk, outer leaves removed, and shredded
- 1 tbsp groundnut oil
- 225 g (8 oz) finely diced pork
- 225 ml (8 fl.oz) chicken stock
- 1 tbsp cane sugar
- 400 ml (14 fl.oz) coconut milk
- the juice and zest of two limes
- 225 g (8 oz) fine egg noodles
- a handful of chopped coriander leaves (optional)

**Serves 4**

1. Finely chop the shallots, chillies and ginger and crush the garlic. Over a medium heat pour the oil in a soup pan and gently fry the shallots and garlic for a few minutes. Add the chillies, ginger, lemongrass and diced pork.

2. Keep stirring until the pork is nicely browned all over. Then add the stock, cane sugar, coconut milk, lime juice and zest.

3. Gently simmer until the pork is cooked, and the soup has thickened slightly.

4. Add the noodles, simmer for 2–3 minutes, remove from the heat, stir in the coriander leaves, if desired, and serve.

French Onion Soup (v)

# French Onion Soup (v)

This vegetarian version of the classic dish replaces the traditional meat stock with vegetable stock and beer to provide the same roundness of flavour. You must use butter, not oil, to caramelise the onions, for the sake of flavour. The 'icing on the cake', is the addition of cheesy croutons floating in the bowl. They absorb the flavour of the soup, and at the same time, disintegrate into it, giving a velvety texture.

## You will need:
- 450 g (1 lb) onions, sliced
- 75 g (2½ oz) butter
- 450 ml (16 fl.oz) draught ale
- 1 tbsp flour
- 2 bay leaves
- 450 ml (16 fl.oz) vegetable stock
- 4 or 5 slices of French bread or ciabatta
- 75 g (2½ oz) grated cheese of your choice

## Serves 4–5

1. Slice the onions finely. Over a medium heat, melt the butter in a saucepan, and fry the onions gently until caramelised, but not burned.

2. Deglaze the pan (p. 43) with a splash of the ale, scraping up all the sticky bits from the bottom of the pan, and then stir in the flour.

3. Cook gently for a few minutes. Add the rest of the ale, the bay leaves and the vegetable stock, and bring to the boil.

4. Turn down the heat, and simmer for about 20 minutes.

5. Depending on the cooking facilities available to you, either prepare 'cheese on toast' with the bread and cheese, and serve this as croutons floating in the soup. Alternatively, to be more authentic, serve the soup in heatproof bowls, float the slices of bread in the soup, sprinkle the cheese over them, and put the whole lot under a hot grill until the cheese is bubbling, and serve.

# Beef and Green Peppers in Black Bean Sauce

# Beef and Green Peppers in Black Bean Sauce

This is always a favourite in Chinese restaurants. You will need a specialist Oriental food store for the salted black beans, which usually come in jars or re-sealable cans. You can also buy them dried, in which case you need to soak them overnight. But if you can't find them, don't worry – use a jar of black bean sauce instead.

**You will need:**
- 2 tbsp salted black beans
- 225 g (8 oz) rump steak, thinly sliced
- 1 tbsp dark soy sauce
- 2 garlic cloves, crushed
- 2½ cm (1 in.) root ginger, finely chopped
- a pinch of Chinese five-spice powder
- 1 tbsp oil
- 4 spring onions, sliced
- 2 green peppers, cut into large cubes

**Serves 3–4**

1. Rinse the black beans, crush them slightly with the back of a fork and put to one side.

2. Marinade the steak in the soy sauce, with the garlic, ginger and five-spice powder (avoid the temptation to use too much five spice powder or it will overpower everything), for at least an hour.

3. Heat the oil in a wok over a high heat, and stir-fry the spring onions for about a minute.

Add the steak and the marinade, and stir-fry for another minute. Then add the black beans and the green peppers and cook for a further minute.

4. The mixture will be quite dry, so add a little cold water to make up a sauce, cook briskly for a few more minutes until thickened and serve.

# Duck with Plum Sauce

# Duck with Plum Sauce

Duck is used extensively in Oriental cooking, and though quite expensive, it goes a long way as it is a very rich meat and can be padded out with plenty of vegetables.

**You will need:**
- 1 tbsp oil
- 2 duck breast fillets, skinned and thinly sliced
- 4 spring onions, diagonally sliced into 1½ cm (2 in.) pieces
- 2 garlic cloves, crushed
- 2½ cm (1 in.) length of root ginger, finely chopped
- 1 tbsp dark soy sauce
- a pinch of Chinese five-spice powder
- 1 star anise
- 200 g (7 oz) tinned water chestnuts
- 1 green pepper, sliced
- 1 carrot, thinly sliced
- 100 g (3½ oz) baby corn, cut in half lengthways
- 6 plums, skinned, pitted and diced

**Serves 3–4**

1. Heat the oil in a wok on a high setting, and quickly brown the duck (about one minute).

2. Add the spring onion, garlic, ginger, soy sauce, five-spice powder and star anise, and stir-fry for a minute or two.

3. Add the rest of the ingredients, turn down the heat and cook until the plums have disintegrated and made a thick sauce. Serve immediately.

# Chicken with Cashew Nuts

# Chicken with Cashew Nuts

The chicken in this dish is marinated in a lemon-based sauce, which perfectly complements the garlic and ginger that is traditionally used in nearly all Chinese stir-fried dishes.

### You will need:

- juice of 1 lemon
- 2½ cm (1 in.) root ginger, finely chopped
- 2 garlic cloves
- 1 tbsp light soy sauce
- 1 tsp cornflour
- 2 chicken breast fillets, thinly sliced
- 1 tbsp oil
- 4 spring onions, cut into 2½ cm (1 in.) pieces
- 100 g (3½ oz) unsalted cashew nuts
- 2 tbsp chopped fresh coriander leaves

### Serves 2

1. Mix the lemon juice, ginger, garlic, soy sauce and cornflour together, and pour over the chicken. Mix well and marinate overnight in the fridge.

2. Heat the oil in a wok over a high heat and briskly stir-fry the spring onions. Add the chicken with its marinade, and stir-fry until the chicken has browned. Add a little cold water to prevent the mixture from sticking to the wok and burning, and to create a thick sauce.

3. Throw in the cashew nuts, heat through and serve garnished with the coriander leaves.

# Pad Thai

# Pad Thai

Thai dishes tend to use naam pla (fish sauce) or shrimp paste for flavouring, although this is primarily for their saltiness rather than a fishy flavour. Pad Thai is a classic dish in which the noodles complement the highly-spiced flavour.

**You will need:**
- 2 garlic cloves, crushed
- 1 stalk lemongrass, chopped
- 2½ cm (1 in.) root ginger, finely chopped
- 4 red bird's-eye chillies, finely chopped
- 1 tbsp naam pla
- juice of 1 lime
- 225 g (8 oz) pork steak, trimmed and thinly sliced
- 150 g (5 oz) fine egg noodles
- 1 tbsp oil
- 2 shallots, finely diced
- 1 tbsp dark soy sauce
- 100 g (3½ oz) unsalted roasted peanuts, coarsely chopped

**Serves 2–4**

1. Mix the garlic, lemongrass, ginger, chillies, naam pla and lime juice together and add the pork. Marinade in the fridge overnight if possible, otherwise for at least a couple of hours.

2. Place the noodles in a heatproof bowl, and cover with boiling water from the kettle.

3. Heat the oil in a wok, and fry the shallots briskly before adding the pork and its marinade. Stir-fry for 4 or 5 minutes, add the dark soy sauce, and a little cold water if it's too dry.

4. Drain the noodles, and add them to the wok, along with the peanuts. Stir to coat the noodles and serve.

**Varition:**
For a meat-free version, leave out the pork, add extra vegetables and substitute the naam pla for light soy sauce.

# Beef Chow Mein

# Beef Chow Mein

Once you've tried this recipe you'll never again eat the greasy stuff that passes for chow mein at most Chinese takeaways.

**You will need:**
- 225 g (8 oz) rump steak, sliced thinly
- 1 tbsp dark soy sauce
- 2½ cm (1 in.) root ginger, finely chopped
- 3 or 4 garlic cloves
- ½ tsp Chinese five-spice powder
- 1 star anise
- 150 g (5 oz) thread egg noodles
- 1 tbsp oil
- 4 or 5 spring onions, cut into 2½ cm (1 in.) pieces
- 1 red pepper, cut into strips
- 1 carrot, sliced thinly at an angle
- 100 g (3½ oz) baby corn, cut in half lengthways
- 100 g (3½ oz) bean sprouts
- 1 tbsp freshly chopped coriander leaves

**Serves 2–4**

1. Put the sliced steak in a bowl with the soy sauce, ginger, garlic, five-spice powder and star anise. Put in the fridge to marinate for at least an hour, but preferably overnight.

2. Place the noodles in a heatproof bowl and cover with boiling water.

3. Heat the oil in the wok and fry the spring onions briefly before adding the steak and its marinade. Stir-fry over a high heat for a minute or two, then add the pepper, carrot and baby corn. Stir-fry for a few minutes, adding a drop or two of cold water to provide some sauce and prevent it sticking.

4. Drain the noodles and add them to the wok along with the bean sprouts. Mix the ingredients together well, add a drop more soy sauce if required, and serve garnished with the fresh coriander if desired.

# Pork with Mango and Lime

# Pork with Mango and Lime

Mango and lime is a combination that works well in sweet and savoury dishes. Thai cuisine tends to use unripe green mangoes in savoury dishes, but ripe ones would work just as well.

**You will need:**
- juice and zest of 2 limes
- 2 garlic cloves, crushed
- 2½ cm (1 in.) of root ginger, finely chopped
- 1 lemongrass stalk, finely chopped
- 1 tbsp naam pla
- 1 tsp ground coriander
- 450 g (1 lb) pork steak, trimmed and thinly sliced
- 1 tbsp oil
- 4 shallots, finely chopped
- 225 ml (8 fl.oz) coconut milk
- 1 mango, diced
- 3 or 4 red bird's-eye chillies, finely chopped
- a lime twist or handful of basil leaves to garnish

**Serves 4**

1. Mix together the lime juice, garlic, ginger, lemongrass, naam pla, and coriander. Add the pork, mix well and marinate in the fridge overnight.

2. Heat the oil in the wok and fry the shallots. Add the pork with its marinade and stir-fry over a high heat until the meat is browned.

3. Add the coconut milk, mango and the chillies, and bring to a simmer. Turn down the heat and cook at a simmer until the sauce has reduced and thickened. Serve garnished with the lime twist or basil leaves.

# Stir-fried Mixed Vegetables (v)

# Stir-fried Mixed Vegetables (v)

Oriental vegetables are now available all year round, due partly to the supermarkets' global economic influences, but also to a few philanthropic organisations that set up projects in developing countries to produce and export such products. By carefully choosing which products you buy you will not only be able to cook delicious meals, but you'll also be assisting third world farmers.

You will need:
- 1 tbsp oil
- 4 spring onions, cut into 2½ cm (1 in.) lengths
- 4 garlic cloves, crushed
- 2½ cm (1 in.) ginger, chopped
- 100 g (3½ oz) mange tout
- 100 g (3½ oz) baby corn
- 100 g (3½ oz) baby asparagus
- 1 red pepper, diced
- 1 courgette, sliced
- 2 tomatoes, skinned, deseeded and chopped
- 1 tbsp dark soy sauce
- freshly ground black pepper

Serves 2

1. Heat the oil in the wok, and fry the spring onions, garlic and ginger on a high heat. Add the mange tout, baby corn, asparagus, pepper and courgette, and stir-fry for a minute or two.

2. Add the tomatoes and cook briskly to evaporate the excess liquid, then add the soy sauce, taste, season with the black pepper and serve.

# Tofu and Baby Corn with Noodles (v)

# Tofu and Baby Corn with Noodles (v)

Tofu, or bean curd, is a soft soya bean product that is widely used across South-East Asia as a meat substitute because of its meat-like texture. It has a fairly bland flavour, and therefore any dish in which it constitutes a major role requires other bold flavours to go with it.

**You will need:**
- 2½ cm (1 in.) of root ginger
- 4 garlic cloves
- 6 spring onions
- 150 g (5 oz) thread egg noodles
- 1 tbsp oil
- 225 g (8 oz) tofu, cubed
- 225 g (8 oz) baby corn, cut in half lengthways
- 1 tbsp dark soy sauce
- 1 tbsp Thai sweet chilli sauce
- 50 g (2 oz) bean sprouts

**Serves 3–4**

1. Finely chop the ginger and the garlic and shred the spring onions.

2. Place the noodles in a heatproof bowl and cover with boiling water.

3. Heat the oil in the wok and fry the garlic, spring onions and ginger briefly on a high heat. Add the tofu, baby corn, soy sauce and chilli sauce and stir-fry for 2–3 minutes.

4. Drain the noodles and add them to the wok along with the bean sprouts. Mix the ingredients together well, heat through and serve.

# Chilli Con Carne

# Chilli Con Carne

Ignore anyone who tries to tell you how to make an authentic Mexican chilli con carne. There is no such thing! The dish is a Texan invention using Mexican cooking techniques and flavourings (also known as Tex-Mex cooking). Some recipes for chilli con carne stipulate the use of chuck steak, but for most people minced beef is perfectly adequate (although buy the best mince you can).

## You will need:

- 1 tbsp oil
- 1 onion, finely chopped
- 5 or 6 garlic cloves, crushed
- 1 tsp ground cumin
- 1 tsp chilli powder
- 450 g (1 lb) steak mince
- 450 g (1 lb) tinned chopped tomatoes
- 3 tbsp tomato purée
- 1 red pepper, diced
- 1 green pepper, diced
- 4 or 5 green chillies, to taste
- 300 ml (½ pt) cold water
- 400 g (14 oz) tinned kidney beans, drained

## Serves 6

1. Heat the oil in a large saucepan, and fry the onion and garlic over a medium heat until softened. Add the cumin and the chilli powder, stir and cook for a moment or two, then add the mince and brown it all over.

2. Add the tinned tomatoes and the tomato purée. Bring to a simmer and add the peppers, chillies and about 300 ml of cold water. Turn down the heat and simmer gently for at least an hour and a half until the mince is tender and has no chewy bits.

3. Add the tin of kidney beans, and cook for another ten minutes.

4. Serve with rice, or in taco shells with sour cream, grated cheese and a side salad.

# Vegetable Chilli (v)

This is an ideal party dish for Halloween or Bonfire Night. Simply make it in the biggest pot you've got, and let everyone help themselves.

**You will need:**
- 1 tbsp oil
- 2 large onions, chopped
- 1 whole garlic bulb, peeled and chopped
- 2 tsp ground cumin
- 2 tsp chilli powder
- 2 large carrots, diced
- 4 courgettes, sliced
- 2 red peppers, diced
- 2 green peppers, diced
- 1 aubergine, diced
- 225 g (8 oz) mushrooms, sliced
- 200 g (7 oz) tomato purée
- 800 g (1 lb 12 oz) tinned chopped tomatoes
- 6–7 green chillies, chopped
- 300 g (10½ oz) tinned sweetcorn
- 800 g (1 lb 12 oz) tinned kidney beans
- 400 g (14 oz) tinned mixed beans and pulses

**Serves 6–8**

1. Heat the oil and fry the onions and the garlic over a medium heat until soft. Add the cumin and chilli powder, stir-fry for another minute.

2. Add the carrots and cook for 4–5 minutes, before adding the courgettes, peppers, aubergine and mushrooms. Stir and cook over a medium heat for about ten minutes.

3. Add the tomato purée, chopped tomatoes and the chillies, and simmer until the vegetables are cooked. Add some water if the mixture looks too dry.

4. Add the sweetcorn, beans and the pulses, and simmer for another 7–8 minutes. Serve with rice or baked potatoes.

# Spicy Mexican Pork

# Spicy Mexican Pork

Pork is an important meat in Mexico as it is cheap to rear and doesn't require prime pastureland (remember, most of Mexico is desert, which is why chilli con carne, using beef, is American, not Mexican). This is an example of the Spanish influence on the cooking of Central America, based on the spicy chorizo sausage.

## You will need:
- 2 tbsp white wine vinegar
- 1 tbsp paprika
- 1 tsp cayenne
- 1 tsp dried oregano
- 450 g (1 lb) minced pork or sausage meat
- 1 tbsp oil
- 1 onion, finely chopped
- 4 garlic cloves, crushed
- 1 tbsp tomato purée

## Serves 2–4

1. Mix together the white wine vinegar, paprika, cayenne, oregano and pork, and leave in the fridge to marinate for at least twelve hours.

2. Heat the oil in a saucepan and fry the onions and garlic over a medium heat, until softened. Add the pork and its marinade to the pan and brown the meat all over.

3. Stir in the tomato purée, and fry the mixture until the pork is cooked. The dish is supposed to be quite dry, so there should not be any need to add liquid; just remember to keep stirring so it does not stick and burn.

4. Serve the meat wrapped up in a flour tortilla, with some sour cream and a side salad.

# Thai Red Beef Curry

Thai curries tend to be classified by colour depending on the ingredient of the sauce; hence red curry contains paprika and green curry, fresh coriander leaves. To be strictly authentic, one should prepare a curry paste, which is then fried with the meat and/or vegetables; this is a quicker, but equally effective version.

## You will need:
- 4 garlic cloves, crushed
- 2½ cm (1 in.) galangal or ginger, chopped
- 1 lemongrass stalk, chopped
- 1 tbsp naam pla
- juice and zest of 2 limes
- 2 tsp paprika
- 1 tsp chilli powder
- 1 tsp ground coriander
- 450 g (1 lb) rump steak, thinly sliced
- 1 tbsp oil
- 4 shallots, chopped
- 1 red pepper, diced
- 1 tbsp tomato purée
- 1 tbsp brown sugar
- 3– 4 red bird's-eye chillies, chopped
- 400 ml (14 fl.oz) coconut milk

## Serves 4

1. Mix together the garlic, galangal, lemongrass, naam pla, lime juice and zest, paprika, chilli powder and coriander. Add the beef and marinate overnight if possible, or for at least two hours.

2. Heat the oil in a large saucepan and fry the shallots for a couple of minutes over a medium heat. Add the beef and its marinade and brown the meat all over. Add the red pepper, tomato purée, brown sugar and chillies.

3. Add the coconut milk and simmer for 10–15 minutes until the coconut milk has reduced, and the sauce has thickened.

4. Serve with delicious, sticky Thai jasmine-scented rice.

# Thai Vegetable Curry with Pineapple (v)

# Thai Vegetable Curry with Pineapple (v)

Pineapple works well in savoury as well as sweet dishes, although for savoury dishes it is best to use fresh pineapple as tinned lacks the firm texture and intense flavour of the fresh fruit. Naam pla is replaced by light soy sauce in this dish for the sake of vegetarians.

## You will need:
- half a fresh pineapple
- 1 tbsp oil
- 4 shallots, finely chopped
- 4 garlic cloves, crushed
- 2½ cm (1 in.) galangal or ginger, finely minced
- 1 lemongrass stalk, chopped
- 1 tsp ground coriander
- 1 aubergine, cubed
- 2 courgettes, sliced
- 2 red peppers, in 2½ cm (1 in.) squares
- 225 ml (8 fl.oz) coconut milk
- 4 red bird's-eye chillies, chopped
- 1 tbsp light soy sauce
- a handful coriander leaves, chopped

## Serves 4

1. Prepare the pineapple by peeling it, removing the core, and cutting it into chunks.

2. Heat the oil in a large saucepan and fry the shallots, garlic, galangal, lemongrass and coriander over a medium heat for a minute or two.

3. Add the aubergine, courgettes, peppers and pineapple and cook for about five minutes, stirring constantly.

4. Add the coconut milk, chillies and soy sauce and bring to the boil. Once boiling, turn down the heat and simmer for five minutes. Stir in the coriander leaves and serve on a bed of rice.

# Chicken Korma

# Chicken Korma

A highly popular, mild Indian curry from the north of the country, cooked in a creamy coconut sauce.

## You will need:

- 4 chicken breast fillets, skinned and cut into chunks
- 225 ml (8 fl.oz) natural yoghurt
- 2½ cm (1 in.) root ginger, finely chopped
- 4 garlic cloves, crushed
- 1 tbsp oil
- 2 large onions, 1 sliced, the other coarsely chopped
- 2 or 3 red chillies
- 1 tsp ground coriander
- 1 tsp garam masala
- ½ tsp turmeric
- 100 g (3½ oz) creamed coconut
- 2 tbsp ground almonds

## Serves 4

1. Marinate the chicken overnight in the yoghurt with the ginger and garlic.

2. Heat the oil in a large saucepan and fry the sliced onion over a medium heat until caramelised. Remove with a slotted spoon and put to one side.

3. Meanwhile, put the coarsely chopped onions in a food processor with the chillies, coriander, garam masala and turmeric and blend to a paste.

4. In the remaining oil in the pan, fry this onion and spice paste for a couple of minutes over a medium heat, then add the chicken and yoghurt mixture. Cook for a few minutes until the meat is browned, then add the creamed coconut and the ground almonds.

5. Cook for about 20 minutes, until the chicken is cooked. Add the sliced onions and a little cold water to thin the sauce if necessary and serve with basmati rice.

# Lamb Madras

# Lamb Madras

This is a fairly hot curry, named after the city of Madras in the south of India, where the climate is hotter. The hot, spicy food helps the locals to keep cool by causing them to perspire more. Lamb is the traditional red meat used in Indian cuisine.

You will need:
- 1 tbsp oil
- 2 onions, finely chopped
- 4 or 5 garlic cloves, crushed
- 2½ cm (1 in.) root ginger, chopped
- 3–4 green cardamoms, split
- 2 tsp ground cumin
- 1 tsp ground coriander
- ½ tsp turmeric
- 1 tsp chilli powder
- ½ tsp powdered fenugreek
- 450 g (1 lb) lamb (preferably leg), trimmed and cubed
- 200 g (7 oz) tinned chopped tomatoes
- 4 or 5 green chillies, chopped
- water or stock

Serves 4

1. Heat the oil in a large saucepan and over a medium heat fry the onions, garlic, ginger, cardamoms and all the ground spices.

2. Add the lamb, and cook until the meat has browned all over. Remember to keep stirring to cook the meat evenly and avoid burning the spices.

3. Add the chillies and stir in. Then add the chopped tomatoes and enough water (or stock) to cover the meat and simmer gently for about an hour and a half, until the lamb is tender and the sauce has thickened. Serve on a bed of rice with naan bread.

# Prawn and Coconut Curry

# Prawn and Coconut Curry

Although fish and seafood tend not to feature much on the average Indian restaurant menu, it is actually widely consumed in India as the country has an immense coastline on some of the most fertile seas in the world. As fish and seafood cooks quickly, the curry sauce is cooked first before the fish is added.

**You will need:**
- 100 g (3½ oz) creamed coconut
- 1 tbsp oil
- 1 onion, finely chopped
- 3 or 4 garlic cloves, crushed
- 2½ cm (1 in.) ginger, chopped
- 1 tsp ground coriander
- 1 tsp ground cumin
- ½ tsp ground fenugreek
- ½ tsp turmeric
- 450 g (1 lb) prawns

**Serves 4**

1. Prepare your creamed coconut by cutting it into small pieces.

2. Heat the oil in a saucepan and over a medium heat fry the onion, garlic and ginger. Add the spices, and fry briefly before adding the creamed coconut and a splash of warm water. Stir constantly, dissolving the coconut into the water, and adding more water as required to make the sauce the right consistency.

3. Add the prawns, stir and cook for a few minutes until the prawns are heated through, but take care not to overcook them or they will become tough and rubbery.

4. Serve on a bed of rice.

# Puddings

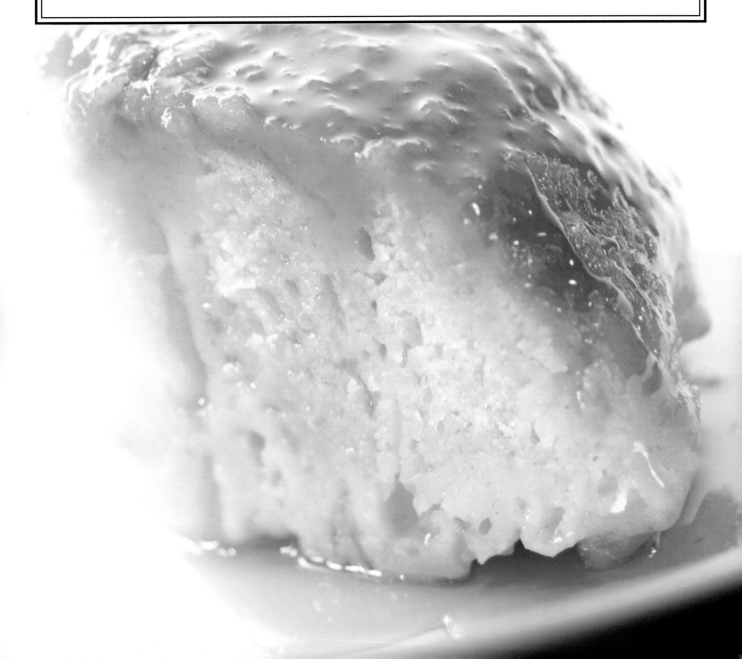

# Steamed Treacle Pudding (v)

Steamed puddings are yet another classic. The choice of flavouring is up to you. This recipe uses golden syrup, but you could use jam, marmalade, lemon juice or lemon curd, raisins or sultanas – or anything else you fancy.

## You will need:
- 25 g (1 oz) butter
- 2 or 3 tbsp golden syrup
- 175 g (6 oz) self-raising flour
- 75 g (2½ oz) vegetable suet
- a pinch of salt
- 50 g (2 oz) caster sugar
- 1 egg
- 90 ml (3 fl.oz) milk

## Serves 4–6

1. Using some of the butter, grease a litre (2.2 lb) pudding basin and put the golden syrup in the bottom of the basin.

2. Mix together the flour, suet, salt and sugar, then beat in the egg and the milk. The mixture should be thick, but not stodgy.

3. Pour the sponge mixture into the basin, and tie a lid of foil or greaseproof paper to the top.

4. Place the pudding basin in a saucepan of simmering water so that the water comes about two-thirds of the way up the side of the basin. Cover the pan, and steam for about an hour-and-a-half to two hours.

5. Turn the pudding out onto a serving plate, and serve with extra golden syrup if required, and cream or custard.

# Rice Pudding (v)

Rice pudding has undergone many transformations and makeovers at the hands of highly-trained chefs. Some cook it on the hob instead of in the oven so it doesn't form a crust. However, rice pudding isn't complete without the 'skin', so this is a traditional recipe.

**You will need:**
- 25 g (1 oz) butter
- 50 g (2 oz) pudding rice
- 450 ml (16 fl.oz) full fat milk
- 25 g (1 oz) caster sugar
- a few scrapes of freshly grated nutmeg

**Serves 4**

1. Use a little of the butter to grease an ovenproof dish. Place the rice in the dish, and pour in the milk. Add the sugar and the nutmeg and dot the butter over the top.

2. Bake in a preheated oven (150°C/300°F/gas mark 1) for two hours, or until the pudding becomes thick and creamy, and has a light golden skin. Do not overcook, otherwise the pudding will be solid and heavy, and the skin will be a horrible crust.

# Bread and Butter Pudding (v)

A few extras can turn an everyday affair into a real treat. This variation of the classic dessert spreads the slices of bread with marmalade as well as butter, and also throws in some candied peel.

**You will need:**
- half a loaf of white bread, sliced
- 50 g (2 oz) butter
- 50 g (2 oz) thick cut marmalade
- 225 ml (8 fl.oz) cream
- 225 ml (8 fl.oz) full fat milk
- 2 large egg yolks
- 100 g (3½ oz) candied peel
- 25 g (1 oz) brown sugar

**Serves 4**

1. Spread the slices of bread with the butter and marmalade, and arrange in a baking dish.

2. Mix the cream, milk and egg yolks to make custard, and pour over the bread, making sure it all gets wet. Scatter the candied peel and brown sugar and bake in a preheated oven for about 40 minutes at 180°C/350°F/gas mark 4, until the top is a golden brown colour.

# Summer Pudding (v)

You can use whatever berries are available, but the usual selection is raspberries, strawberries, blackberries, blackcurrants and redcurrants.

**You will need:**
- 900 g (2 lb) of seasonal berries and currants
- 100 g (3½ oz) caster sugar
- half a loaf of white bread, sliced with crusts removed

**Serves 4–6**

1. Place the fruit in a saucepan, over a low heat with half the sugar, stirring occasionally until the fruit is soft and the juices are running. Remove from the heat and allow to cool.

2. Line a basin with the bread slices, leaving enough bread to make a lid for the pudding, and pour in the fruit, reserving a little juice. Scatter with the remaining sugar. Cover the fruit with the rest of the bread, and pour over the reserved juice.

3. Place a plate on top of the pudding and refrigerate overnight. To serve, remove the plate, place a serving dish upside down over the pudding, and carefully invert the whole lot.

# Chocolate Chip Ice Cream (v)

Ice cream is not difficult to make, and you don't need an expensive ice cream maker; just some very basic kitchen equipment and a freezer. But for this recipe you must buy decent quality chocolate with at least 70 per cent cocoa solids.

**You will need:**

- 1 vanilla pod
- 225 ml (8 fl.oz) double cream
- 75 g (2½ oz) caster sugar
- 3 eggs, separated
- 100 g (3½ oz) dark plain chocolate, chopped into chips

**Serves 4**

1. Split the vanilla pod carefully with a knife so that the flavours will infuse the dish.

2. Place all the ingredients, except the chocolate and the egg whites (but including the yolks), into a bowl over a pan of simmering water, and whisk until the mixture forms a thick custard. Turn off the heat. Remove the vanilla pod, scrape the seeds of the pod into the custard and discard the rest.

3. While the custard is cooling, beat the egg whites until stiff, and then fold into the custard. Do not add the chocolate at this stage, as the mixture requires stirring several times during the freezing process.

4. Put the mixture in a plastic tub with a sealable lid, and put in the freezer. After two hours, remove from the freezer, and whisk the ice cream, to break up the ice crystals. Repeat after another two hours, but this time add the chocolate chips as well. Return to the freezer for several hours, until it is firm.

# Chocolate and Vanilla Ice Cream Loaf (v)

Don't be confused by the fact that a 450 g (1 lb) loaf tin is supposed to accommodate 900 g (2 lb) ice cream. Ice cream is much denser than bread, so the weight of bread required to fill a tin would be less than the weight of ice cream required to fill the same tin.

**You will need:**
- 225 g (8 oz) plain chocolate (70 per cent cocoa solids)
- 450 g (1 lb) good quality vanilla ice cream
- 50 g (2 oz) chopped hazelnuts
- 450 g (1 lb) chocolate ice cream
- 175 ml (6 fl.oz) double cream, whipped
- 225 g (8 oz) digestive biscuits, crushed
- 50 g (2 oz) butter

**Serves 4–6**

1. Melt the chocolate in a bowl over a pan of simmering water.

2. Grease the inside of the loaf tin with a little of the vanilla ice cream and scatter the hazelnuts in the tin, so that they are evenly distributed over the bottom and sides.

3. Build up layers of chocolate and vanilla ice cream in the tin, drizzling some melted chocolate, and spooning in some of the whipped cream in between each layer.

4. Mix the crushed biscuits with the butter so that it forms a firm crust to lie on top of the ice cream (forming a base for when it is turned out) and press it down gently, without squishing the ice cream too much.

5. Put in the freezer for a couple of hours, and remove ten minutes before serving.

# Apple Tarte Tatin (v)

For this recipe you will need a pan that you can use on the hob and in the oven; a frying pan with a metal handle would be ideal.

**You will need:**
- 2 large cooking apples
- 50 g (2 oz) unsalted butter
- 50 g (2 oz) caster sugar
- 300 g (10½ oz) puff pastry
  (chilled pastry from the supermarket is fine)

**Serves 4**

1. Peel and core the apples, and cut into thin wedges. Slice the butter and distribute evenly over the bottom of the pan. Sprinkle over the sugar and arrange the apple slices in an overlapping pattern.

2. Roll out the pastry, and cut a circle that will fit the pan. Put the pan on a moderate heat until the butter and sugar begin to caramelise. Remove from the heat, allow to cool slightly and lay the pastry over the top, tucking the edges down into the pan.

3. Put in a preheated oven at 200°C/400°F/gas mark 6 for 20 minutes, until the pastry has risen and turned brown. Remove, allow to cool slightly, and turn out onto a plate.

# Tropical Fruit Salad (v)

The fruit you use in this salad will depend on what is available. Supermarkets tend to stock a good range of exotic fruits all year round and specialist shops will stock more weird and wonderful fruit. However, avoid tinned fruit as the key to this salad is freshness.

**You will need:**
- 1 pineapple
- 2 mangoes
- 2 papayas
- 1 honeydew melon
- 2 kiwi fruit
- 2 bananas
- juice and zest of 4 limes
- 2 tbsp dark brown sugar
- 100 ml (3½ fl.oz) dark rum

**Serves 4–6**

1. Peel, deseed, core and generally prepare the fruit and cut them all into convenient, bite-sized pieces. Put them in a large bowl with the lime juice and zest, the sugar and the rum.

2. Marinate for at least 12 hours in the fridge before serving.